MULTIPLYING MOVEMENTS

Multiplying Movements

© 2021 by Forge. All rights reserved.
Published by Forge, 14485 East Evans Avenue,
Denver, Colorado 80014

ISBN 978-0-578-30031-3 (paperback)
ISBN 978-0-578-30033-7 (e-book)

Cover Design by Lauren Atherton.

Written by Forge Speakers and Staff.

Visit us online at www.forgeforward.org

CONTENTS

LAUNCHING INTO THE MULTIPLYING MOVEMENTS VISION

**Today,
you have the opportunity to begin living
a world-changing life of impact!**

CORRESPONDING VIDEOS

You can find and purchase all the videos designed to accompany this booklet on the Forge App or at MultiplyingMovements.com

The harvest truly is plentiful and the laborers few (Matthew 9:37-38). There are *not enough people* to meet the needs of the world, *not enough people* to bring the message of Jesus to the lost, *not enough people* to fulfill what Jesus sent us to do. Our world needs people who live with *hearts on fire* for Jesus and *lives on purpose* for His Kingdom!

You can be the difference our world needs! You live in harvest fields no one else does. You have the opportunity to live a world-changing life of impact!

———

The question is, will you?
Will you take up the cause?

———

We will never reach the world and fulfill the very heartbeat of God if we do not become Kingdom laborers and multiply others to be and do the same. We must pass on to others what has been shared and entrusted to us (2 Timothy 2:2).

With this vision in mind, *Multiplying Movements* is not only meant to be received but passed. It is designed for your heart to catch fire and for you to begin living a life on purpose, so that the fire can spread! … A wildfire is coming!

As you progress through *Multiplying Movements*, you will be challenged and equipped to train others using this tool—whether that's other believers who need this tool too or others that you lead to Christ.

So, will you commit to spiritual multiplication? Will you commit to fulfilling the prayer request of Jesus by not only becoming a laborer through *Multiplying Movements*, but also, using *Multiplying Movements* to mentor others and equip them to become laborers too?!

You might be thinking, *I'm not even sure what a laborer does. I'm not sure that I have what it takes.* If that's what is going through your mind, don't worry! That's why this tool exists. All that matters at this point is your willingness to say, "Yes, I want to become a multiplying laborer."

————

Today, I commit that I will use the *Multiplying Movements* tool to become a Kingdom laborer, and seek to multiply others to do the same:

Signature: _____

Date: _____

TIPS FOR MENTORING & MULTIPLYING

Each time you meet with a small group or individual that you are leading through *Multiplying Movements*, follow this model:

- Set a time to meet regularly (doing the same time weekly is recommended).

- You have several options on how to incorporate the videos when multiplying and mentoring others, whether in a small group or one-on-one:

Have the group or person you are mentoring watch the episode and process the "Now What?" questions at the end of each chapter before meeting with you so that they are prepared to engage.

Or, watch the episode together, provide some space for each person to process the questions, and then discuss them together. You may even decide to create your own additional discussion questions if you are using *Multiplying Movements* in a Bible study or small group format.

If you are watching these videos together, we recommend using the **web version of the app*** which can be accessed at MultiplyingMovements.com. The web version of the app is fully functional and can be viewed in larger formats (such as full screen on a computer or connected to a TV or projector).

* A quick note on how to get the most out of accessing the web version of the app using a desktop or laptop computer:

On your <u>computer</u> web browser (not your phone or tablet), go to MultiplyingMovements.com and click "Access Web Version." The link will take you to a page that has a QR Code on the left (for putting the app on your phone or tablet) and a picture of a phone on the right. The phone, however, is so much more than a picture—it's a fully functional app you can interact with (click it and see!).

*On the interactive app of the phone, click the "Multiplying Movements" box and you will be able to view all the videos **full screen** by clicking the expansion icon in the right corner once the video appears.*

Lastly, the web version of the app can be accessed from a phone or tablet in addition to a computer. Just know that on a phone or tablet, the web version will function like a normal app.

- Read and discuss the key Scripture(s) together (at the top of each message outline).

- Review the main message content with them. Ask them what stuck out or resonated with them most. Make sure they understood the key points of the message.

- Ask if they have any questions related to the topic. And, be prepared with some questions you can ask to help them process further.

- Review the "Now What?" section from the previous week. Ask them how they did with their steps of obedience last week.

- Share a story or example of something from your life related to the topic in order to challenge or encourage them.

- Encourage them to pray for and engage the lost, as laid out in the messages. Ask them who they are praying for and who they are engaging.

- Encourage them to utilize the tool to mentor others in the same way they are receiving the content. Ask them who God is leading them to mentor. Check up on how that is going.

- Pray together.

OTHER HELPFUL RESOURCES:

Baton Passing Relationships (booklet)
by Dwight Robertson

For purchasing options and more resources, go to:
MultiplyingMovements.com

1

THE VISION: BECOMING KINGDOM LABORERS

Matthew 9:35-38

**Do you want your life
to make an _____ on this world?**

Jesus was focused on seeking and saving the lost, and His strategic plan was more Kingdom Laborers in every facet and sphere of society worldwide!

JESUS' MINISTRY MODEL & STRATEGY:

Up-_____

You may impress up front, from a distance. But you impact up-close.

"The harvest is plentiful" (Matthew 9:35-38)—there are too many people without hope and without purpose. There is a lot of work to be done, so pray for more harvest hands!

In the _____ of everyday life

Outside the synagogue/church: workplaces, recreation locations, where you live.

One _____ at a time

Domino-ripple effect… More time with less people causes greater impact.

JESUS' MINISTRY METHOD:

_____ – Take note of the people around you.

_____ – Slow down enough to truly engage others.

_____ _____ _____ – Life transformation often happens when we spend time with others life-on-life, up-close. This often happens at meal tables!

Love is spelled ___ ___ ___ ___.

A KINGDOM LABORER IS SOMEONE WHO...

- Strategically follows Jesus' method of impacting others.

- Sees, Stops, and Spends time with others.

- Loves God with everything and loves others, 24/7 every day and everywhere.

YOUR OBSTACLES

"I'm too imperfect."

We don't need to look to ourselves, but rather just need to point to the one who is _____!

"My sin struggle has disqualified me. I'm too unworthy."

You have not lost your value to God. Welcome to the unworthy club; He is the _____ one!

"I don't have enough training."

Has Jesus shown up for you? If so, you have _____-_____ to tell. Jesus has worked through ordinary people time and time again! (Acts 4:13)

"I'm too afraid."

Pray the Ten-Finger prayer: "I can do all things through _____ who strengthens me."

NOW WHAT?

Commit to becoming a Kingdom Laborer:

Write down your prayer commitment to God here (something like "Lord, I commit to becoming a Laborer for your Kingdom. I desire to make a lasting impact!").

Starting this week, where and with who can you begin to see, stop, and spend time with?

What are your potential obstacles? List them here and talk to God about them:

Commit to Multiplying Your Impact:

(This tool is meant for you, but not only for you! God desires to multiply your impact through others.)

Who are the people that God might want you to begin mentoring using this *Multiplying Movements* tool? Write their names here, and then this week ask them to get together sometime. When you get together, discuss meeting regularly to go through *Multiplying Movements* (this might be one-on-one or a small group of friends – whatever you are more comfortable with).

List ALL the people in your life who do not know Jesus yet (they might be people you know very well or distant people who you have not learned their name yet). Starting right now, begin to regularly pray for them:

OTHER HELPFUL RESOURCES:

Plan A: And There is No Plan B (book and audio)
by Dwight Robertson

For purchasing options and more resources, go to:
MultiplyingMovements.com

NOTES
The Vision: Becoming Kingdom Laborers

THE STARTING PLACE: DEVELOPING A HEART ON FIRE

Matthew 22:37

Everyone is in one of four chairs.
The goal is getting in chair ___.

CHAIR 1: ON FIRE

SOMEONE WHO COMPLETELY AND TOTALLY LOVES _____. (John 14:15, Luke 10:27)

People do crazy things when they are in _____! People around you can tell what you love by the way you act and live.

The person in chair one:

- Reads the _____.
- Spends time praying.
- Shares their faith.
- Is full of the _____ of the Lord, even in suffering and persecution. (Nehemiah 8:10)

CHAIR 2: LUKEWARM

SOMEONE WHO BELIEVES IN JESUS BUT HAS BECOME COMPLACENT.

The person in chair two:

- Has gotten _____ to God.
- Goes half speed for Jesus.
- Is more focused on how they feel than what God thinks of their worship.
- Is self-focused.
- Hypocritically living in sin but acting differently in church and around other believers.

"You have left your first _____." (Revelation 2:2-4)

How we treat our family reveals what we think about Jesus.

(Ephesians 5:22-6:4)

Chair two is "_____" to Jesus. (Revelation 3:15-20)

CHAIR 4: UNBELIEVER

SOMEONE WHO DOES NOT BELIEVE IN JESUS.

The person in chair four knows for a fact they are not a

_____.

CHAIR 3: UNKNOWINGLY LOST

SOMEONE WHO THINKS THEY ARE SAVED BUT ARE NOT.

This chair is the most spiritually dangerous place to be!

The person in chair three:

- Has possibly prayed a prayer, been baptized, or joined a church but they never truly trusted in Christ.
- Is not bothered by their _____; they have no conviction of _____.
- Has no spiritual fruit or life change.

HOW DO YOU GET TO CHAIR ONE?

If you are in chair four: Tell Jesus you are sorry for your sin and give your life to Him!

If you are in chair three: You need to give your life to Jesus. If you are not sure whether you are in chair two or three, then give yourself fully to Jesus and make sure! Tell Jesus, "I am sorry for my sin and I give you everything I am."

If you are in chair two: Tell Jesus, "I want to return to my first love. I am sorry for my sin and I want to re-surrender everything I am to you."

Jesus _____ for us, so we should _____ for Him!

NOW WHAT?

Prayerfully Consider which chair you have been in.

Write it down here, and why you think that is the chair you have been in:

If you have been in chair 2, 3, or 4, are you ready to move to chair 1? If you are, take some time to write a prayer of commitment below. If not, take some time to write out why you are not ready to commit to being a "chair 1" follower of Jesus.

Take these reasons to God in prayer. We encourage you to make this decision soon—don't wait. Even if you have apprehensions, Jesus can help you through these difficulties.

Write your prayer commitment to Jesus here:

Starting this week, what specific next steps can you take to develop your heart on fire for Jesus and live in chair 1?

Jesus has always called his followers to proclaim what He has done in their lives, even from the very moment they encountered Him (see Mark 5). People who encounter Jesus most often experience some kind of change as a result (such as new peace, joy, freedom from a sin or addiction, hunger for God's Word, etc).

Maybe you experienced some of these changes today while making a commitment to become a "chair 1" Christian. With that in mind, will you commit to regularly telling others how Jesus has changed your life?

Write down some ways encountering Jesus has changed your life:

Starting this week, who can you tell about how Jesus has shown up in your life? Consider the people you have begun praying for in your life who do not yet know Jesus.

Write their names here in the order you hope to share with them. As you're able, continue sharing with 1-5 people weekly!

1. _____
2. _____
3. _____
4. _____
5. _____

Remember, at the start of this journey, you committed to becoming a *multiplier*. Have you begun to meet with others and mentor them using this tool? It is time to begin meeting with them! If you have not yet, take some time now to reach out to a few people that you can begin to train using this tool.

OTHER HELPFUL RESOURCES:

8 Marks of a Disciple Bible Study (booklet and messages) by John Vermilya

For purchasing options and more resources, go to:
MultiplyingMovements.com

NOTES
The Starting Place: Developing a Heart on Fire

_____

_____

_____

_____

_____

_____

_____

_____

_____

_____

_____

_____

_____

SEEKING GOD INTIMATELY

Genesis 5:21-24

**The more _____ I spend with Jesus,
the more I get to _____ Him.**

WALKING WITH GOD

Enoch _____ with God. (Genesis 5:21-24)

In the Bible, the word "walking" is often equivalent to

_____.

You can enjoy fellowship with God anywhere you go, as a lifestyle!

We can _____ God by enjoying fellowship and spending time with Him. (Hebrews 11:5-6)

SEEKING GOD

Rewards of Seeking God:

Getting to _____ God.

Listening to God's Words and understanding His plans.
(Jude 1:14-15)

Seeking God through _____:

Read with purpose and expectation.

You can read in chronological order, or read specific books, or search specific topics.

Meditate on and dig into Scripture by asking questions.

Write in your Bible or write on post it notes.

With the purpose of getting to know Jesus.

Seeking God through _____:

Come with a list of prayer requests.

Talk to God on the go, all the time, wherever you are, and whatever you are doing.

Enjoying and Worshiping Jesus:

Sit with God, walk with God, hike with God.

Make room to listen for His voice.

Journal what God is doing, your prayers, etc.

Pray out loud.

Praise the Lord and sing to Him.

Spending Extended Time with God through a Day or "Date" Alone with God (DAWG):

Find a location without distractions.

Bring fun snacks (if you are not fasting).

Bring your Bible.

Bring your journal.

Bring worship music.

NOW WHAT?

We often schedule important appointments and times to meet with friends, but we fail to prioritize meeting with God. What if you took some time right now to schedule an EXTENDED Date Alone With God (DAWG)? We promise, you wont regret it!

Write down the date, time, and place you plan to spend time with God:

Date:

Time:

Place:

It's critical to our spiritual life to spend time alone with God every day. What time will you daily commit to seeking Jesus? What do you desire your daily time with God to look like?

While it is crucial to spend time alone with God, He goes with us in our daily lives. Starting today, begin to engage and enjoy Jesus throughout your daily on-the-go schedule. Brainstorm and write down some ways you can remind yourself of God's presence as you go throughout your day:

OTHER HELPFUL RESOURCES:

Is God Waiting for a Date with You? (booklet)
by Dwight Robertson

Forged by Fire (book and audio)
by Dwight Robertson

Awakening: a 40-day Journey toward Deeper Intimacy with God
by John and Shannon Boyd

Practicing God's Presence: Brother Lawrence for Today's Reader
by Robert Elmer

For purchasing options and more resources, go to:
MultiplyingMovements.com

NOTES
Seeking God Intimately

NOTES
Seeking God Intimately

4

ENGAGING THE WORD OF GOD

2 Timothy 3:16-17

**What if we committed our lives to learning
God's Word and ways every day?**

WHY WE GET INTO GOD'S WORD

**If God's Word truly became the authority on which we base our
lives:**

**We would grow in firsthand _____ with God, which
brings both joy and awe.**

Too often, we have based our relationship with God primarily
on other people's close relationship with God.

We would learn to hear, know, and _____ His voice.

We follow Jesus in a world of competing _____, so we must seek God's voice based on His Word. (John 10:27)

We must be compelled first by God's _____, then live out our faith based on His truth, and lastly engage emotion only after (not before) His truth!

We must memorize God's Word, allowing it to flow in and through our lives.

HOW WE GET INTO GOD'S WORD

Every time you open the Bible, use the following model in order to dig into the Scripture and allow it to permeate your life...

Practicing Together:
Mark 2:1-12

_____ – **What does the passage say?**
(What do you learn about God, Jesus, the Holy Spirit, people, sin, evil, etc.)

_____ – **What is God speaking to you from this passage?**
(Is something from the passage really jumping out to you? Is there a sin you need to confess, a life example you want to follow, etc.?)

_____ – **What will you do about it this week?**
(How can you specifically and practically obey Jesus this week based on what He showed you in the text?)

_____ – Is there someone you can share this truth with this week?

Is there a verse you should memorize?

TIPS ON GETTING STARTED

- Choose a book of the Bible to read through one passage per day, until you complete that book. Consider starting with the book of Mark as it is the most simple book of the Bible on the life of Jesus. After Mark, dig into Acts to discover how Jesus' followers lived. After Acts, move onto Ephesians to fully comprehend the gospel message and who we are called to be as followers of Jesus. After Ephesians, continue to read various books of the Bible until you have read every single book.

- Use the **Head, Heart, Hands, Feet** model (from above) each time you read so that you fully engage God's Word with your entire life. (James 1:22-25)

- As you read, choose verses and sections to memorize.

- Write down any questions you have about the passages you read and discuss them with a mentor.

- If you can, use a physical, paper copy of the Bible (studies have proven reading physical copies rather than electronic copies increases retention), and write in your Bible: star, underline, draw, highlight etc.

NOW WHAT?

Honestly evaluate your time in the Bible and select where you currently are:

_____ I read the Bible daily.

_____ I read the Bible 4 or more times per week.

_____ I read the Bible 1-3 times per week.

_____ I read the Bible 2 times per month.

_____ I read the Bible 1 time per month or less.

What is getting in the way of you engaging God's Word more often?

Consider this incredible reality: A recent study by the Center for Bible Engagement found that those who read the Bible four or more times a week (compared to those who read the Bible less than four times a week) had significantly decreased loneliness, significantly increased victory over sin struggles (such as anger, bitterness in relationships, pornography, drunkenness, sex outside of marriage, etc.), and significant increases in sharing the gospel and discipling others.

Pray now and ask, "Lord, will you increase my hunger for your Word?"

Choose a book of the Bible and engage the first passage, practicing *Head, Heart, Hands, and Feet* right now; and commit to continuing this practice in your daily time with God...

OTHER HELPFUL RESOURCES:

Spiritual Life Notebook (Bible Study section)
by Forge

For purchasing options and more resources, go to:
MultiplyingMovements.com

NOTES
Engaging the Word of God

5

PURSUING PASSIONATE PRAYER

Matthew 6:9-13

Prayer is a lifestyle and a conversation. God wants to move us from being people that pray to becoming people *of* prayer!

"Lord teach us to pray." (Luke 11:1-5)

People of Prayer, Pray Regularly

Jesus often withdrew to pray. (Luke 6:12)

Prayer needs to be _____ regularly.

How to P.R.A.Y.

P_____ – Reminding ourselves of who God is as we tell Him who He is. Praise completes our enjoyment, and lifts us to see from God's perspective.

R_____ – God shines His light into our lives to fully address our hearts, cleansing them from sin and darkness. We must confess our sin and forgive those who have wronged us.

A_____ – Receiving the truth of who God is in our lives, as we seek Him for our needs. Receiving requires asking (James 4:2-3). God desires to bless us with spiritual "riches" in Christ as we ask Him.

Y_____ – "not my will but your will be done." Sometimes God will say "no" to things we ask for because He knows what is best, and He has a plan that we do not always know. Yet, we must trust and submit to Him in all things. More than our own plans and desires, we must desire to see Jesus' Kingdom cause occur in and through our lives.

When to Pray (James 5:13-18)

- When we experience _____ and hardship.

> *"God whispers to us in our pleasures,*
> *but He screams at us through our pains."*
> – C.S. Lewis

- When everything is going well.

- When we are _____ or weary.

... We are to pray in *all* circumstances! (Ephesians 6:18)

Prayer is not only talking; it also includes listening. This happens through God's Word and also through the Spirit, because we carry God's presence everywhere we go!

People of Prayer, Pray _____

- We can't pray passionately because we don't pray

  _____.

- If we do not pray specifically, we never really witness God's answer to our prayer.

- When you pray specifically and witness God answer, it builds your _____ and gives God _____ …

- … as this happens you will become more passionate in prayer! (Luke 11:5-10)

People of Prayer, Pray in _____

"Elijah was a man just like us"—God answers the specific prayers of ordinary people who pray in faith, believing that God will answer!

Spirit-Led Scripture-Fed Prayer time: Praying the very Word and _____ of God.

- You can stand on faith knowing that what God has said He will do, He will do!

- There are 8,000 promises in God's Word.

- You can hold onto God's promises in prayer, trusting that He will answer!

NOW WHAT?

Take some time to talk with God using the P.R.A.Y. acronym right now (Praise, Repent, Ask, Yield). Commit to practicing prayer in your daily time with God.

Listening Prayer Tips – Prayer is a conversation that includes both talking and listening. Consider these common ways that God speaks to us (seen throughout Scripture).

- **The Bible**: God always communicates to us through the plain meaning of Scripture and also through Scripture penetrating our hearts based on our specific circumstances (2 Timothy 3:16).

- **Whispers**: The still small voice of God often comes in thoughts that are not our own but from the Holy Spirit (Mark 13:11; Acts 8:29; Acts 13:2).

- **Pictures**: Dreams as we sleep or visions that we see while awake, almost as if they are in our imagination, can be from God (Acts 16:9-10; Acts 2:17; Acts 10:9-20).

- **Burdens**: You may feel heavyhearted or compelled by God that you must do something (Jeremiah 20:9; Matthew 9:36; Luke 19:41-46).

Grab a journal. Pray, asking the Lord in Jesus' name to silence your flesh and the enemy. Ask God to speak to you, and ask that you hear His voice alone. Maybe you have a specific question, or maybe you just want to ask if God has anything to say to you.

Listen. Write down whatever comes to mind. Make sure it is truly God speaking by confirming what you heard aligns with the teaching of the Bible, that it comes with the peace of Christ, and that it glorifies God not yourself.

Receive whatever you hear God saying. And when applicable, commit to obey it. Make this a regular practice in your life!

Begin praying specifically, seeking God and His Word for ways that He might be leading you to bring specific requests to Him. In your journal, draw a vertical line down the center of the page—on the left side write "prayer requests" and on the right side write "answers."

Regularly write down your requests on the left along with the date. Continue to go back and pray for those things, writing down the answer in the right column when you witness God resolve your request.

OTHER HELPFUL RESOURCES:

Spiritual Life Notebook ("Prayer Requests" journal section)
by Forge

Awakening: a 40-day Journey toward Deeper Intimacy with God
by John and Shannon Boyd

For purchasing options and more resources, go to:
MultiplyingMovements.com

NOTES
Pursuing Passionate Prayer

_____

_____

_____

_____

_____

_____

_____

_____

_____

_____

_____

_____

_____

NOTES
Pursuing Passionate Prayer

6

PARTICIPATING IN THE LOCAL CHURCH

Acts 2:42 • 1 Corinthians 14:26 • Ephesians 4:12

**The Church is a gathering of God's people,
built on the truth of who Jesus is.**

This is the first time in Scripture we see the word "_____."
(Matthew 16:18)

The Church will be built on the truth who Jesus is, the Christ, the
_____. (1 Peter 2:6)

The Church is: a _____ of God's people.

Jesus said, "I will build _____ Church"

Jesus is claiming ownership of the Church. It is His responsibility to build a church and to shut one down.

Many have tried to stomp out the Church for over 2,000 years, but they have not succeeded.

If You Are a Christian, You Go to Church

- We need the church for our _____.

- We need the church to worship with other believers.

- We need the church to be equipped to scatter for ministry.

- We need the church to help resolve our conflict with other believers. (Matthew 18:15-20)

Believers Gather for... (Acts 2:42)

_____ – God's Word.

_____ – Relationship with other believers; we are not meant to live in isolation.

_____ ___ _____ – Communion, commemorating the death and resurrection of Jesus.

_____ – Communicating with God together, praying with and for one another; and bringing your tithe/giving as offering and prayerful worship to God.

God has given various giftings in the church to equip every ordinary believer to do the work of the ministry. (Ephesians 4:12)

We gather for worship and then _____ for ministry.

The church is not a building or a location, but a local _____ of believers who come together as God has commanded. (Hebrews 10:25)

NOW WHAT?

Are you involved in a local church? Why or why not?

Jesus is calling you to get involved and engage the local church. If you are not already engaged in a local church, you need to find a church or start a church.

FINDING A CHURCH

What to look for in finding a church:

- First and foremost focused on Jesus (not political or social issues, etc.).
- Actively engaging God's Word (the Bible).
- Focused on engaging God's mission/the great commission. (Matthew 28:18-20)
- Includes the practices of Acts 2:42.

STARTING A CHURCH

Maybe there are no churches in your area, or God is leading you to start one. Here are some tips on launching a "church" gathering:

- It does not have to be complicated. You can meet weekly in your home with just a few believers and grow from there.

What do you do when you gather?

- Provide opportunity for everyone to engage the practices of Acts 2:42 when you meet—engage God's Word together (that could even be more discussion focused), pray together, remember the death and resurrection of Jesus together (communion), and build meaningful relationships (that might mean you have meals together).

- Regularly encourage participation and allow space and time for various people to engage and participate in the gathering as the Lord leads, as seen in 1 Corinthians 14:26.

- Regularly encourage believers to lovingly engage the lost in their everyday life, eventually inviting them into the church when they come to believe or when they are willing to join.

Have you been criticizing the church without offering solutions? How so?

- Pray and ask for God's forgiveness if you have been complaining.

- Rather than criticizing from the outside, how can you begin to serve and be a part of the solution to the potential problems you see?

Use your spiritual gifts to serve the local church:

What are your spiritual gifts? (Romans 12:6-8; 1 Corinthians 12:7-11, 28; and Exodus 31:1-6).

This week, take a **spiritual gifts assessment**, which can be found in the "Other Helpful Resources" section.

After prayerfully studying these scriptures, asking God how He has created you to serve His Kingdom, and taking the spiritual gifts assessment, list your spiritual gifts here:

After completing the above assignment, prayerfully brainstorm how you can use your gifts to serve your local church. Consider meeting with the appropriate leaders or mentors in your church setting and ask how you can use your gifts to serve and be a blessing.

OTHER HELPFUL RESOURCES:

Now What? Practical Tips to Fuel Your Faith (booklet) "Chapter 5: Hanging Out with Other Christians," by Forge

For purchasing options and more resources, go to:
MultiplyingMovements.com

NOTES

Participating in the Local Church

NOTES

Participating in the Local Church

（7）

REDISCOVERING THE GOOD NEWS

I Corinthians 15:1, 3-4

**What does the Scripture say
is most important?**

The _____ is of first importance. So, what exactly is it?

"Gospel" means _____ _____.

"Good news" was used to announce kings in great military victories in ancient times. In the gospel, Jesus is announced as the new king!

So, how did Jesus unveil His kingship?...

Christ died for our sins

We are born _____ from God because of our sin. (Isaiah 59:2)

Sin leads to _____. (Romans 3:23)

No one can cross the gap to God. The sin chasm is too wide.

Therefore, _____ comes to us, paying the price for our sin!

Jesus took our place and our penalty for our sin, to bring us to God. (1 Peter 3:18)

Christ was buried

Jesus could not have survived Roman flogging and crucifixion. The Romans were expert executioners.

Jesus really was _____. He truly did take on the punishment for our sin.

Three days later Christ raised from the dead

Jesus really did rise from the dead, not just spiritually but physically.

Jesus' resurrection is the most important moment in history!

Jesus' _____ is the "lynchpin" of Christianity.
Without it, everything falls apart. Without the _____,
we don't have Christianity. (1 Corinthians 15:14)

With the resurrection, we have the most amazing news ever
told!

If Jesus really did rise from the dead:

- All of our _____ is worthwhile.

- Our faith is founded on the rock, who is Jesus.

- The death of Jesus really did pay the price for our _____.

- We will be resurrected too when Jesus returns.

- We can be filled with joy, peace, and contentment.

Jesus appeared to many people, proving His resurrection and power
to transform lives! (1 Corinthians 15:5-8)

The Good News!

Jesus died for our sin, was buried, and rose from the dead,
revealing that He really is the one true King and Lord of all.

The good news should affect _____ aspect of our life:

- We must know it, understand it, and share it.

- Our relationships should reflect the good news of Jesus and His love. (Ephesians 5-6)

- Embracing the good news impacts how we invest our money for the Kingdom.

- The good news should impact the choices we make.

- The good news is for every day of the week, for every moment.

NOW WHAT?

Before this teaching, how would you have described the "gospel" or the "good news"? Did it shift at all based on this message? How so?

What aspects of the good news do you need to spend more time digging into? How can you engage that aspect more fully?

Has the good news fully impacted every aspect of your life? Where do you need to allow God to more fully impact you—any key relationships? Your finances? Your choices in this season of life? How you invest your time?

OTHER HELPFUL RESOURCES:

Now What?: Practical Tips to Fuel Your Faith (booklet)
by Forge

For purchasing options and more resources, go to:
MultiplyingMovements.com

NOTES
Rediscovering the Good News

OVERCOMING HINDRANCES

Hebrews 12:1-4

Throwing off everything that hinders to run our unique races of loving God, loving others, and advancing His Kingdom!

It is like we are running a race with chains holding us back...

WHAT "CHAINS" MIGHT BE HINDERING US?

_____ **Sin** (1 John 1:9)

- Our sin is often rooted in pride, evil desires, and division.

- Rather than confess our sin we often choose to live in darkness.

_____ **Lies** (John 8:32)

- When we don't know the _____, we begin to believe lies.

- When we are not engaging the _____, we begin to believe lies.

_____ (Colossians 3:13)

- We are to forgive those who wrong us in the same way that God has forgiven us in Christ.

- When we don't forgive, it is like a wound that begins to fester with disease and becomes worse. Our healing begins with _____.

_____ **Relationships** (1 Corinthians 15:33)

- Anyone in your life having a stronger influence in your life than God Himself...

- Children dishonoring and disobeying your parents, wives not submitting to your husbands, husbands disrespecting and not loving your wives in the same way Jesus did the Church, physical intimacy outside of marriage.

_____ Patterns (1 Peter 1:18)

- An empty way of life, sin, and negativity passed down to you from your family.

- Jesus has set us free from this but we often walk in old ways rather than in the newness of life.

Spiritual _____ (James 4:7)

- Satan is seeking to attack believers (Ephesians 6:16; 1 Peter 5:8), especially those who are obeying Jesus and laboring for His Kingdom. (Revelation 12:9, 17)

- When we don't submit to God and resist the enemy's attacks, the devil may gain a place of influence (a foothold) in our lives. (Ephesians 4:26)

5 Weapons of our Warfare:

1. Scripture out loud. (memorize scripture!)

2. The name of Jesus out loud.

3. The armor of God. (Ephesians 6:10-17)

4. Prayer.

5. Praise.

HOW DO WE THROW OFF EVERYTHING THAT HINDERS?

Above all, look to _____! …then begin to do what His Word teaches us:

- Confess your sin.

- Rebuke lies and receive God's truth.

- Forgive those who have wronged you.

- Rebuke negative generational patterns and embrace God's plan for your future.

- Leave behind unhealthy relationships and seek Godly ones.

- Rebuke the enemy's attack in your life: "In Jesus' name go away!"

It is for freedom that Jesus has set you free; do not be _____ all over again! (Galatians 5:1)

Will you choose the chains
or the freedom
that Jesus has purchased for you?

NOW WHAT?

Spend some time now and ask Jesus, "What are the chains hindering my life right now?" Write them here:

Continue in prayer, dealing with each chain that you have recognized is in your life. Do what God's Word teaches us to do with each one of these hindrances.

Dealing with our chains is not a "one and done" event. We must continue throwing off *everything* that hinders throughout all of life. Continue looking for chains that might begin hindering you from this day forward. Deal with them immediately in prayer!

OTHER HELPFUL RESOURCES:

"Spiritual Warfare" message
by Charlie Marquis.

This message will help you dig deeper into the topic, including helpful ways to pray through spiritual warfare in your life.

For this resource and many more, go to:
MultiplyingMovements.com

NOTES
Overcoming Hindrances

NOTES

WALKING BY FAITH

Hebrews 11:1-12

Joining Jesus on a Kingdom-advancing adventure, full of meaning and purpose!

The Journey of Living by Faith...

FOUNDATIONAL FAITH

Whoever receives Him, becomes a child of God.

Your relationship with God began with you responding to His initiative.

At this stage, you begin establishing an understanding of His ways and your inheritance in Christ.

God is _____ you up and deepening your roots. (Colossians 2:6-7)

Yet, Jesus invites us beyond foundational faith into an adventure full of meaning and purpose... Jesus doesn't want us to just be well-taught but well-_____.

**A CALL
TO FAITH**

THE CALL

What does this call to adventure and impact, to faith-walking look like? How do you know it's God?

- There will most often be a _____ of God's prompting.

- It will often be confirmed through _____.

- It will often be affirmed by objective, godly others.

A life of faith is not about how much information we can pack into our brains, not about how well-taught we are, but how well-walked we will be. It's about taking action and joining the adventure.

THE INTERNAL BATTLE

As God asks you to step out and step forward, fear and obstacles will come at you trying to pull you back.

At times, people around you will even ask you how this will really work out?

- Your response: "___ _____ _____. I may not have the answer, but I do have assurance that this is what I am supposed to do, and I know that God must know. It is mine to trust Him."

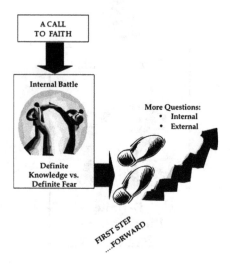

THE FIRST STEP FORWARD

Don't think you know how to do this. Let _____ direct your steps and the entire journey. Let Him show you how—all along the way.

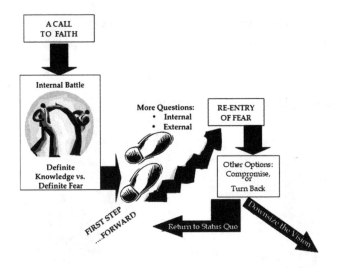

THE RE-ENTRY OF FEAR

- Fear _____ and doubts.

- Fear needs every _____ in place but that's not possible because you are walking by faith.

- Fear requires a high false security.

Practice Proverbs 3:5-6 as you walk forward in what God is calling you to do!

Fear cannot be your _____!

If you allow fear to be your leader, it will tell you to:

- Compromise and down-size the vision.

- Turn and run.

At this point in the faith journey, often out of necessity, you will go deeper with God.

Do not look logically at what can happen.

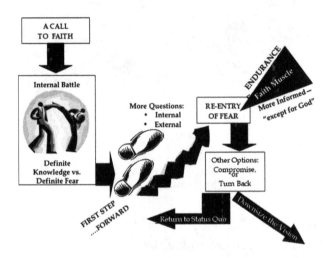

ENDURANCE

Fix your eyes on _____, who endured (Hebrews 12:3), so that you can endure!

- Remember who your _____ is.

- Focus on who your God has been for others in history.

- Remember the _____, and hold onto God's promises.

- Remember your earlier days (when you faced a challenge and witnessed God come through).

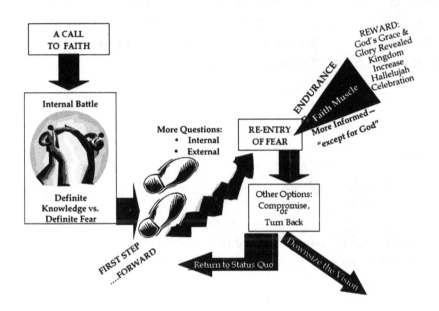

THE REWARD OF WALKING BY FAITH

- God's grace and glory revealed.

- Kingdom increase.

- Hallelujah celebration!

"_____ _____, good and faithful servant."

NOW WHAT?

Spend some time in prayer right now asking God, "How do you want me to step out in faith, joining you in a Kingdom adventure?" Write down anything that comes to mind—whatever God burdens your heart with or whatever dreams for the world He brings, no matter how big or impossible they may be:

When you think about what God might be calling you to do, what fears arise? Write them down and give them over to God in prayer.

Continue to look for God's reoccurring prompting (whether in the Word, in prayer, through others, etc.). As they come, write down and journal any potential confirmations or leadings, so that you do not forget, and so that your faith and confidence in Him are built up!

What is one way that you can take a step of faith this week?

OTHER HELPFUL RESOURCES:

It's My Turn: 20 Kingdom Laborers Who Changed Their World and Compel Me to Impact Mine (book)
by Forge

For purchasing options and more resources, go to:
MultiplyingMovements.com

NOTES
Walking by Faith

NOTES
Walking by Faith

10

UTILIZING YOUR YOU-NIQUE MINISTRY

Ephesians 2:10

**Meeting people at their point of need,
using the uniqueness of our lives.**

WHAT IS MINISTRY?

_____ is meeting people at their point of need.

Ministry happens in real life, in real space, with real people, and is meeting real needs.

Each one of us should use whatever gift we have received to _____ others. (1 Peter 4:10)

Outside of church gatherings, there are _____ plus hours in the week to live out ministry as unique as you are.

Just like David did not fit in Saul's armor, each of us do not fit perfect "ministry" molds.

- Each of us have unique God-given _____.
- God has designed you with a ministry purpose in mind.

HOW TO DISCOVER YOUR UNIQUE ABILITIES AND MINISTRY PURPOSE:

1. Ask God, your creator-designer.

2. Get into the _____ and allow God to show you His plan.

You will see and notice things others don't see. Ministry can look like you!

GOD DESIRES TO EMPLOY YOUR _____ LIFE FOR HIS MINISTRY PURPOSES:

- Using your uniqueness, you will reach people no one else can? No pastor nor missionary is positioned to reach the people God is asking *you* to reach!

- God can employ your _____ and your spiritual gifts.

- God can employ your _____ and interests.

- God can employ your God-story.

- God can employ the _____ you go: where you work, where you live, where you recreate, wherever you go daily.

- God can employ your _____ _____.

- God can employ your tragedy, pain, and suffering.

NOW WHAT?

Spend some time praying right now. Ask God to help you see unique ministry opportunities that He has created you for.

Fill out the Personal Ministry Inventory (below).

Do a quick inventory of the things in your life that God can employ in "ministry."

One of the greatest joys in life comes when we live out God's purpose for us. He has designed each of us like no other and His design is perfect for ministry. Perhaps that's why God seems to give us the entrepreneurial freedom to creatively apply our gifts and passions to ministry.

What could ministry look like if it's as distinct and unique as you are? We challenge you to do an inventory of the things in your life that God can employ in ministry. It could help you discover more about how God can employ "who you are" to minister to others "where they are."

What Does Ministry Look Like?

Often, we have a tendency to believe that to be in ministry, we must be a pastor, missionary, musician or some other "typical" ministry vocation.

But, that's just not the case. God has created each of us uniquely to carry out the distinct ministry He's called us to. We can use our gifts, passions, hobbies and interests for the Kingdom.

What is unique about you that can be used for the Kingdom?

PERSONAL MINISTRY INVENTORY

What are your hobbies and/or recreational interests?

- ☐ Fly Fishing
- ☐ Cooking/Baking
- ☐ Running/Working out
- ☐ Skateboarding
- ☐ Gardening or lawn work
- ☐ Investing
- ☐ Traveling
- ☐ Motorcycling/Bicycling
- ☐ Knitting/Sewing
- ☐ Painting
- ☐ _____
- ☐ _____
- ☐ _____

What season of life are you in?

- ☐ Student
- ☐ Professional
- ☐ Early Married
- ☐ Parents of Young Children
- ☐ Parents of Teenagers
- ☐ Empty Nester
- ☐ Retired
- ☐ _____
- ☐ _____
- ☐ _____

What financial/physical resources do you have to offer?

☐ Tithe
☐ Savings/Investments
☐ Property
☐ Transportation
☐ _____
☐ _____
☐ _____

What are some life experiences you've had?

☐ Travel experiences
☐ Job experiences
☐ Relationship experiences
☐ Educational experiences
☐ _____
☐ _____
☐ _____

What are some painful life experiences?

☐ Cancer Survivor
☐ Loss of child or other family member
☐ Injury
☐ Spiritual Struggle
☐ Dark night of the Soul
☐ Loneliness
☐ _____
☐ _____
☐ _____

What are your spiritual gifts?

(refer to your spiritual gifts test results)

- ☐ Leadership
- ☐ Service
- ☐ Teaching
- ☐ Mercy
- ☐ _____
- ☐ _____
- ☐ _____

Do you have any special skills?

- ☐ Mechanical
- ☐ Hospitality
- ☐ Art/Photography/Videography
- ☐ Music
- ☐ Carpentry
- ☐ Writing
- ☐ Caregiving
- ☐ Sports
- ☐ Education
- ☐ Gardening
- ☐ Camping/Hiking/Outdoors
- ☐ Conversation/Communication
- ☐ Scrapbooking
- ☐ Organization
- ☐ _____
- ☐ _____
- ☐ _____

Where and When Does Ministry Happen?

Think about it for a second... ministry happens in the ordinary venues of life. Not only overseas, in a church or during a camp meeting. Here are some examples:

☐ With our families
☐ At our church
☐ At work
☐ In our neighborhoods

Community events
While doing yard work
Block parties
Our neighbors and their interests

_____

☐ At school

Dorm
Locker
Classes
Events
Student Union

_____

☐ In our communities

Clubs
Civic Organizations
Parent-Teacher Organizations
Boards
Rescue Missions
Ministry Organizations

_____

☐ Along the Way

Grocery Store
Restaurant
Bank
Gas Station
Post Office

**Where are the ordinary venues
in *your* life?**

Stepping Outside Your Comfort Zone

Are you willing to take a step of faith, to go outside of your comfort zone, to minister for God simply because you love Him?

If you answered "yes" (even a timid "yes" counts), then here are a few examples how you can step outside your comfort zone:

☐ Going "out of your way" to reach others
☐ Putting yourself in unfamiliar places of outreach
☐ Using newly-developed gifts
☐ Changing locations or taking financial faith steps
☐ Serving in ways that seem "lowly"
☐ Serving in ways that cause you to sacrifice
☐ What are some other ideas you have?

Next Steps

Now that you've begun to identify what ministry can look like (your unique hobbies, interests and passions) and you know where and when ministry can take place (the ordinary venues in your life), here are some next steps to help you carry out your unique and distinct ministry.

Look back at your inventory and see how your unique hobbies, interests and passions can be specifically applied to ministry in your life situations.

- Prayerfully ask God to give you opportunities for ministry.

- Take time to search the scriptures for verses about your giftings. Take note how others in the Scriptures use a similar gift-sets to glorify God and reach others.

- Read a book about your area of unique ministry.

- Talk to a trusted Christian friend, parent, mentor or spiritual leader about your unique, everyday ministry idea. Brainstorm together how you can use your uniqueness to glorify God and minister to others.

- Make a list of the people and places that could benefit from your ministry.

**What will you do this week to begin
connecting with others
using your YOU-nique ministry?**

OTHER HELPFUL RESOURCES:

Plan A: And There is No Plan B (book and audio)
by Dwight Robertson

For purchasing options and more resources, go to:
MultiplyingMovements.com

NOTES
Utilizing Your YOU-nique Ministry

11

REACHING THE LOST

Mark 16:15 • Colossians 1:26-27

**We need to tell as many people
as we can about Christ!**

Adam and Eve before the fall: _____, without sin.

Adam BEFORE the Fall

Adam and Eve after the fall: Sinful.

Adam AFTER the Fall

Sin has dominion over them (arrows up). This is the reality for all of humanity after them.

Those who believe in Jesus: Victorious.

NORMAL CHRISTIAN

Sin no longer has dominion. It is still present, but it has been crucified. (arrows down)

What is in the circle?! ...

God goes to _____ _____ to bring the lost to Himself!

Extreme Measure #1 – _____ from Heaven. (1 Kings 18)

Extreme Measure #2 – _____. (Jonah)

Extreme Measure #3 – _____. (fell to the ground and grew the tree that became the cross of Christ)

… There are a lot of extreme measures throughout the Scriptures.

Final Extreme Measure…

_____ in you. (Colossians 1:26-27)

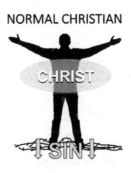

The _____ _____ in you. (Ephesians 1:13-14)

The _____ in you. (John 14:23)

The Father, Son, and Holy Spirit are all three _____ you!

———

_____ **are the extreme measure of God!**

———

You are the most powerful entity on this planet.
That's why we need to tell as many as we can about _____!

WHAT DOES IT LOOK LIKE TO TELL OTHERS ABOUT JESUS?

A very practical and powerful way to tell others about Jesus is to share our stories of what He has done in our lives. What would that look like?

- Share what your life was like before encountering Jesus. What difficulty did you face? What negative things did you experience? What misconceptions did you have about God?

- Share how you encountered Jesus—what did that time look like, and what led to it? (Prayer time, someone told you, etc.)

- Share about how Jesus changed your life. What is now different in your life because of Jesus? What is the real change Jesus has brought? Maybe you're wondering, what if I believed in Jesus when I was really young and don't have a before/after story? Your story might be your salvation experience, but it might also be a post-salvation experience when Jesus really showed up for you and changed your heart or circumstances.

- After you share your story, share the simple gospel message in this practical way: "This was possible in my life because Jesus died on the cross for our sins, which separated us from the one true God. Jesus then rose from the dead, so He is alive today and waiting for relationship with us. He loves us! And do not forget to end with a question: "Is this something you are interested in? Do you want Jesus to change your life too?"

We can share anywhere, anytime, with anyone. We can share our Jesus-stories in just a short couple minutes.

VARIOUS RESPONSES TO JESUS

What do we do with the various ways people might respond when we share?...

"I am ready to follow Jesus."

Pray together with them right then! Say something like this to encourage them to begin a relationship with Jesus, "Why don't you pray out loud with me right now and tell Jesus something like this in your own words: 'Jesus, I believe you died on the cross for my sin and rose from the dead. Today I want to begin a relationship with you. I submit my life to follow you.'" (This concept comes from Romans 10:9)

Once someone believes in Jesus, begin going through this *Multiplying Movements* tool with them starting at Episode 1 so that they too can become a laborer for God's Kingdom!

"I do not want to follow Jesus. I am not interested."

If someone is not ready to follow Jesus and not interested in learning more, then simply continue to love them in action, continue to share different stories of Jesus at work in your life as you get the chance, and most importantly keep praying!

"I'm not ready to follow Jesus yet, but I'm interested in learning more."

You might find someone fumbling a little bit between being ready to follow Jesus and unsure if they are ready. If this is the case, you can ask a simple question like "What is holding you back from following Jesus?" and then discuss whatever that is.

It could be that this simple conversation removes their obstacle to following Jesus and they decide to believe!

In other cases, they might need more time before deciding to follow Jesus. If this is the case, ask them to begin meeting with you regularly to explore what Jesus is all about and discuss any questions they may have.

MEETING INSTRUCTIONS FOR THOSE INTERESTED BUT NOT READY TO FOLLOW JESUS

When you meet, follow the order of the list of Bible stories below and discuss one passage each time you meet. Read the passage together and discuss it simply in this way:

What did you learn about God?
(You can consider using these questions too: What did you learn about humanity? Or about evil?). After discussing, you may also share about the theme of the story as outlined in parenthesis throughout the Bible stories schedule below.

If this story is true, how can you apply the story to your life?
(The final story will lead them to an opportunity to believe in Jesus, after learning the overall story of the Bible).

This is the list of stories you will use each time you meet:

Old Testament

Genesis 2:4-25
(Creation: God's creation reveals His goodness and that He desires relationship with humanity)

Genesis 3:1-21
(The Fall: Impact of sin on the world yet God still promises His provision - see especially verses 15 and 21)

Note: You might consider skipping the remainder of these Old Testament stories and going straight to Jesus in the New Testament (unless your context calls for these stories up front).

Genesis 6:5-14; 7:1-5; 7:18-23; 8:1-3; 8:15-22
(Noah: God's provision must be received)

Genesis 12:1-5; 22:1-14
(Abraham: God's heart is for people of every nation and tribe in the world and God provides a sacrifice for the sin of them all)

Exodus 3:1-17
(Moses: God sees and responds to the suffering of His people)

Daniel 3:8-30
(Shadrach, Meshach, and Abednego: God is faithful and rescues His people)

New Testament

Matthew 1:18-25, plus reference prophecy in Isaiah 7:14
(The Birth of Jesus: the coming savior for all the sins of the world)

Mark 4:35-41
(Jesus calms the storm and He can calm all "storms" in our lives)

Luke 8:26-39
(Jesus has power over darkness and evil spirits)

Mark 5:25-34
(Jesus has power over sickness)

Luke 7:11-17
(Jesus has power over death)

Luke 10:38-42

(Jesus reveals what is most important in life: life up-close to Jesus)

Luke 10:25-37

(Jesus defends the weak, and teaches what is most important for His followers: loving God and loving others)

Mark 7:14-23

(Jesus teaches what is sinful)

Luke 5:18-26

(Jesus has power to forgive sins)

Mark 15:21-39, or extended using 14:43-15:47

(Jesus dies for our sins)

Matthew 28:1-10

(Jesus rises from the dead and his followers worship Him)

John 9:1-7; 9:18-38; Romans 10:9

At the end of this story, discuss in this way:

"We see 3 responses to Jesus: deny Jesus like the religious leaders, believe secretly but not confess him like the parents, believe and confess Jesus publicly like the blind man. Who do you want to be more like, the religious leaders, the parents, or the man born blind?"

Based on their response ask them if they want to publicly confess Jesus and follow Him. If they say yes, then pray with them to begin a relationship with Jesus and begin using *Multiplying Movements* together, beginning with Episode 1.

NOW WHAT?

How does your perspective change, realizing that the Father, Son, and Holy Spirit are all inside of you, and that YOU are the extreme measure of God?

Write down the three parts of your Jesus-Story and combine them:

Practice your Jesus-story along with the basic gospel message (Cross and resurrection), and an ending question ("Are you interested in this?").

Review your list of lost people from Episode 1: Becoming Kingdom Laborers. Who will you tell beginning this week?

Continue to share your Jesus-story with people on your "lost list," and tell people week by week everywhere you go.

OTHER HELPFUL RESOURCES:

Christian Man Laws (book)
by Adrian Despres

For purchasing options and more resources, go to:
MultiplyingMovements.com

NOTES
Reaching the Lost

NOTES
Reaching the Lost

12

EMBRACING GOD'S HEART FOR THE WHOLE WORLD

Matthew 28:17-20

**From the very beginning to the end,
God's heart has always been for the whole world, for all nations.**

OUR GOD-GIVEN PURPOSE

God had chosen Israel to be a Kingdom of Priests for _____
_____. (Exodus 19:6)

- Israel was chosen to _____ the one true God to the
rest of the world.

- God desires for people from all nations to know and worship
Him. (Isaiah 56:6)

- Yet, Israel failed to fulfill their God-given purpose. (Mark
11:15-17)

In the Bible, the word _____ does not mean geo-political countries. Rather, it refers to tribes or ethno-linguistic people groups.

God has chosen us as _____ to proclaim Him to the world. (1 Peter 2:9)

STATS: THE STATE OF THE WORLD, MISSIONS, AND THE CHURCH

61% of Christians have never shared their faith (Lifeway Research)

42% of the world's population belongs to an unreached people group (3.14 billion people) … (The Traveling Team Statistics)

- **Lost**: unbelievers who live in "Christianized" places are not unreached. They are lost.

- **Unevangelized**: unbelievers who are part of a people group or tribe with a Christian population higher than 2% but live in regions with absolutely no Christians, are considered "unevangelized."

- **Unreached**: a tribe/ethno-linguistic people group that is 0-2% Christian and has no ability to sustain Kingdom movement.

- **Frontier**: a people group with 0% Christianity.

- **Unengaged**: a people group with 0% Christianity, and no one attempting to bring the gospel to them.

83% of the unsaved do not have access or opportunity to hear about Jesus. (The Traveling Team Statistics)

Of 400,000 cross-cultural missionaries only 3% go to the unreached. (The Traveling Team Statistics)

For every 1 unreached people group, we have 900 churches and 78,000 evangelical Christians... *There are roughly 7400 unreached people groups in the world! (The Traveling Team Statistics)

For every $100,000 of Christian income, only $1 goes toward initiatives for the unreached. (The Traveling Team Statistics)

51% of church attendees in the U.S. were unfamiliar with the term "Great Commission"...

> ... 25% or respondents said they heard of it but did not recall its "exact meaning" (Barna Research Group)

> ... That means that at least 76% of church attendees are clueless regarding God's burning passion for the unreached of the world!

The Great Commission: "Go make disciples of ____ _____."
–Jesus (Matthew 28:17-20)

- His final command must become our _____ concern!

- The Great Commission is not an option to be considered, but a _____ to be obeyed. –Hudson Taylor

---

WHY ARE WE FAILING TO FULFILL OUR GOD-GIVEN PURPOSE?

We may feel:

- Too inadequate.
- That we don't know _____.
- That we don't have enough training.
- That Kingdom impact is for Church leaders and _____ people.

  But, God can use _____ people to change the world! (Acts 4:13)

We might be:

- Too afraid.
- Lazy.
- Ignorant.
- Disobedient.

HOW DO WE ENGAGE GOD'S HEART FOR THE NATIONS?

3 Types of Christians (Romans 10:14-15)

- _____

- Senders

- _____

Which one are <u>you</u>?

A few ways you can participate as a *Sender*:

• _____.

• Give.

• _____ goers.

• Leverage your unique _____ and _____.

  - *Business branch, platform, or name.*
  - *Invent creative mission resources or mission technology.*
  - *Use computer skills to help get the gospel into restricted systems.*
  - *Spread the story of God's Kingdom movement through photography and videography.*

A few ways you can prepare and participate as a *Goer*:

• Take a _____ _____ mission trip.

  - *Be exposed to the unreached and great harvest needs.*
  - *Build relationships.*
  - *Share the gospel.*
  - *Discover what God is up to among the nations.*

• Research mission _____ that match you and your calling so that they help train and prepare you to launch out as a missionary to the unreached.

• Research and study other religions.

- *Understand their beliefs.*
- *Apologetics.*
- *How to build bridges to their culture and beliefs.*
- *Evangelism and discipleship tactics.*

• Find refugees and immigrants from unreached people groups near your city.

- *Go meet them, build relationships, find ways to love them, and share the gospel.*

• _____ for the unreached of the world and consider where God is sending you!

- *Check out JoshuaProject.net and PeopleGroups.org (click on the interactive maps and look for the red dots – most unreached people groups of the world).*

- *Prayerfully consider going to the most unreached places so that you can change the future of the statistics you discovered in this message!*

Jesus will build His Church,
even in the spiritually darkest places on the planet,
and He will not be _____!
(Matthew 16:13-20)

OTHER HELPFUL RESOURCES:

Mudrunner: Advancing the Kingdom No Matter the People, the Place, or the Cost (book) by Charlie Marquis

For purchasing options and more resources, go to:
MultiplyingMovements.com

NOTES
Embracing God's Heart for the Whole World

NOTES

Embracing God's Heart for the Whole World

_____

_____

_____

_____

_____

_____

_____

_____

_____

_____

_____

_____

ANSWER KEY

Chapter 1 - The Vision: Becoming Kingdom Laborers
impact, close, mainstreams, life, See, Stop, Spend Time With, T I M E, perfect, worthy, God-stories, Christ

Chapter 2 - The Starting Place: Developing a Heart on Fire
1, Jesus, love, Bible, joy, used, love, puke, Christian, sin, sin, died, live

Chapter 3 - Seeking God Intimately
time, know, walked, lifestyle, please, know, Scripture, Prayer

Chapter 4 - Engaging the Word of God
friendship, obey, voices, truth, Head, Heart, Hands, Feet

Chapter 5 - Pursuing Passionate Prayer
practiced, Praise, Repent, Ask, Yield, suffering, sick, Passionately, specifically, faith, glory, Faith, promises

Chapter 6 - Participating in the Local Church
Church, Cornerstone, gathering, MY, souls, Teaching, Fellowship, Breaking of Bread, Prayer, scatter, gathering

Chapter 7 - Rediscovering the Good News
gospel, good news, separated, death, Jesus, God, dead, resurrection, resurrection, preaching, sin, every

Chapter 8 - Overcoming Hindrances
Unconfessed, Believing, truth, Bible, Unforgiveness, forgiveness, Unhealthy, Generational, Warfare, Jesus, enslaved

Chapter 9 - Walking by Faith
building, walked, reoccurrence, Scripture, I don't know, God, calculates, answer, leader, Jesus, God, Scriptures, Well done

Chapter 10 - Utilizing Your You-nique Ministry
Ministry, serve, 160, abilities, Bible, whole, talents, hobbies, places, past experiences

Chapter 11 - Reaching the Lost
perfect, extreme measures, Fire, Whale, Seed, Christ, Holy Spirit, Father, inside, You, Christ

Chapter 12 - Embracing God's Heart for the Whole World
all nations, represent, nations, Christians, all nations, first, command, enough, up-front, ordinary, Goers, Disobeyers, Pray, Encourage, gifts, talents, short term, organizations, religions, Pray, overcome

MORE FORGE OPPORTUNITIES FOR YOU

ForgeForward.org

FORGE SPEAKERS & EVENTS
ForgeSpeakers.com

Needing someone to challenge your group to become passionate followers of Jesus who live with hearts on fire and lives on purpose? Forge has the right speaker for your next event!

FORGE EQUIPPING PROGRAMS for ALL AGES
ForgeForward.org/Equipping

Forge Equipping is not summer camp and training events "as usual." Forge challenges and equips people of all ages to become you-nique, lifelong Kingdom laborers in everyday places and beyond.

FORGE BOOKS & RESOURCES
ForgeForward.org/Resources

Looking for a deeper relationship with God and hands-on practical ways to widen His Kingdom impact through your life? Forge has the resources to help get you actively laboring in God's Harvest fields.

FORGE VIDEO CONTENT
Subscribe to free video content at Youtube.com/ForgeForward

FORGE PODCAST
FuelForTheHarvest.com

FORGE DAILY TEXTS
Text SPARK to 33222 for one-sentence daily devotionals

NEEDING PRAYER?
Email us at Prayer@ForgeForward.org

CONTACT US
FORGE: Kingdom Building Ministries
14485 E. Evans Ave.
Denver, Colorado 80014

303.745.8191
info@forgefoward.org

Ordinary people everywhere are joining
God's Kingdom movement.
Are you ready to start laboring & multiplying God's Kingdom harvest?